Untamed Horizons: Extraordinary Tales of Oceania's Resilience, Diversity, and Wonder

Welcome to "Untamed Horizons: Extraordinary Tales of Oceania's Resilience, Diversity, and Wonder." In this eBook, we invite you on a captivating journey through the vast and enchanting region of Oceania, where remarkable stories unfold and inspire. From the lush islands of Polynesia to the rugged landscapes of Australia and New Zealand, and the cultural richness of Melanesia and Micronesia, Oceania is a tapestry of diverse peoples, breathtaking natural wonders, and extraordinary human achievements.

In this collection of case studies, we delve into the untold stories that have shaped the history, culture, and spirit of Oceania. These tales reflect the resilience of its people, the richness of its traditions, and the awe-inspiring landscapes that have left an indelible mark on the world. Each story is a testament to the human spirit, highlighting tales of triumph, exploration, preservation, and innovation.

Join us as we uncover the tales of courageous voyagers, ingenious navigators, indigenous wisdom keepers, environmental stewards, and remarkable individuals who have defied odds and overcome challenges. Through these narratives, we aim to celebrate the diversity of Oceania's peoples, honor their remarkable achievements, and inspire readers with the extraordinary stories that lie within this vast and captivating part of the world.

Embark on this literary journey, where you will witness the untamed horizons of Oceania come to life, inviting you to explore, reflect, and be captivated by the remarkable tales that await. Open your mind, expand your horizons, and let the spirit of Oceania guide you as we unveil its extraordinary stories of resilience, diversity, and wonder.

The Journey of Eddie Mabo

The Journey of Eddie Mabo is a remarkable story of a man who fought tirelessly for Indigenous land rights and made a significant impact on Australian history. Eddie Koiki Mabo was born on Murray Island in the Torres Strait in 1936. His journey began when he became aware of the unjust land ownership system in Australia, which denied the rights of Aboriginal and Torres Strait Islander peoples to their traditional lands.

In the 1970s, Eddie Mabo started to challenge the legal doctrine of terra nullius, which stated that Australia was unoccupied land before British colonization and therefore belonged to the Crown. Mabo firmly believed that his people, the Meriam people of the Murray Islands, had a continuous connection to their ancestral lands and deserved recognition and ownership rights.

Eddie Mabo's fight for justice led to a historic legal case known as the Mabo Case. In 1982, Mabo, along with other plaintiffs, took their case to the High Court of Australia. After a decade-long legal battle, the High Court delivered its landmark decision on June 3, 1992. The court recognized the existence of native title, overturning the concept of terra nullius and acknowledging the rights of Aboriginal and Torres Strait Islander peoples to their traditional lands.

The Mabo decision was a pivotal moment in Australian history. It not only recognized the rights of Indigenous peoples to their lands but also highlighted the need for reconciliation and the acknowledgment of Australia's Indigenous heritage. Eddie Mabo's determination and courage paved the way for subsequent legal and legislative reforms in land rights and Indigenous affairs.

Tragically, Eddie Mabo passed away from cancer just months before the High Court ruling. However, his legacy lives on, and he is remembered as a fearless advocate for justice and equality. His journey inspired countless individuals and communities across Australia and had a profound impact on the recognition and preservation of Indigenous culture and rights.

The Mabo decision sparked a national conversation about land rights and reconciliation. It led to the introduction of the Native Title Act in 1993, which established a framework for the recognition and protection of native title rights in Australia. The act acknowledges the ongoing connection of Indigenous peoples to their lands and provides a process for negotiating land rights claims.

The journey of Eddie Mabo serves as a powerful reminder of the importance of standing up for justice and the impact that one person's determination can have on the lives of many. His story continues to inspire and educate people about the ongoing struggles faced by Indigenous peoples and the importance of recognizing and respecting their rights.

The legacy of Eddie Mabo is celebrated through events such as Mabo Day on June 3rd each year, which commemorates the historic High Court decision. His journey remains a symbol of resilience, hope, and the ongoing pursuit of justice for Indigenous peoples not only in Australia but around the world.

The Polynesian Voyagers

The Polynesian Voyagers were ancient seafarers who navigated the vast Pacific Ocean using only their knowledge of the stars, currents, and natural landmarks. They embarked on daring voyages that spanned thousands of miles, connecting the scattered islands of Polynesia and shaping the history and culture of the region.

The origins of the Polynesian Voyagers can be traced back over 3,000 years ago when they began their explorations of the Pacific Ocean. Using double-hulled canoes known as wa'a, the voyagers set sail from their home islands, guided by their deep understanding of celestial navigation and the environment. These canoes were marvels of ancient engineering, capable of withstanding the powerful swells and strong winds of the open ocean.

The Polynesian Voyagers had an intimate relationship with nature and relied on their keen observations of the stars, the movement of ocean currents, the flight patterns of birds, and the behavior of marine life to guide their journeys. They developed a sophisticated understanding of how to read the signs of the ocean, allowing them to navigate between islands with remarkable accuracy.

One of the most famous voyages undertaken by the Polynesian Voyagers was the settlement of Hawai'i. It is believed that they sailed from the Marquesas Islands, over 2,000 miles away, using their navigational skills to navigate across the vast expanse of the Pacific. These voyages required immense courage, skill, and knowledge, as they ventured into uncharted waters for weeks or even months at a time.

The Polynesian Voyagers not only sought new lands but also carried with them the seeds of their culture, language, and traditions. Through their explorations, they established connections and cultural exchange between islands, shaping the Polynesian identity that persists to this day. They brought with them knowledge of agriculture, fishing techniques, and social systems that helped sustain their communities in the new lands they settled.

The legacy of the Polynesian Voyagers extends beyond their remarkable seafaring abilities. Their journeys demonstrated the vast capabilities of ancient peoples and their resilience in navigating and settling the remote islands of the Pacific. Their navigational techniques, passed down through generations, continue to be practiced and celebrated in Polynesian cultures today.

In recognition of their accomplishments, the Polynesian Voyagers are revered as heroes and symbols of cultural identity and exploration. Their voyages embody the spirit of adventure, discovery, and the deep connection between humans and the natural world. The Polynesian Voyagers remind us of the remarkable achievements of ancient civilizations and the importance of preserving and honoring their rich heritage.

The Story of Te Puea Herangi

Te Puea Herangi was a prominent Māori leader and advocate for the rights and welfare of the Māori people in New Zealand. Her life story is a testament to her unwavering commitment to her people and her tireless efforts to preserve Māori culture and improve the living conditions of her community.

Born in 1883, Te Puea was a member of the Tainui tribe, with ancestral connections to the Waikato region in the North Island of New Zealand. From a young age, she demonstrated strong leadership qualities and a deep understanding of the importance of preserving Māori heritage and traditions.

Te Puea's leadership skills were further honed through her involvement with the King Movement, a Māori political and cultural movement that sought to protect Māori rights and authority. She played an active role in supporting King Mahuta, who was the paramount leader of the movement at the time.

During the early 20th century, Te Puea witnessed the devastating impact of colonization on her people. Māori lands were confiscated, and traditional practices were suppressed. Te Puea saw the urgent need to revitalize Māori culture and empower her people to reclaim their land and heritage.

One of Te Puea's notable achievements was the establishment of Tūrangawaewae Marae in Ngaruawahia, a significant gathering place and cultural center for the Māori people. The marae became a symbol of Māori resilience and a hub for community activities, cultural events, and political discussions. Te Puea's leadership and vision helped create a space where Māori traditions and values could be celebrated and passed on to future generations.

During the Great Depression in the 1930s, Te Puea's compassion and determination became even more evident. She worked tirelessly to provide food, shelter, and employment opportunities for those in need, particularly Māori families who were disproportionately affected by the economic downturn. She advocated for the establishment of Māori schools and vocational training centers to empower Māori youth and equip them with the skills needed for a better future.

Te Puea's legacy extends beyond her lifetime. She inspired future generations of Māori leaders and activists to continue the work she started. Her commitment to social justice, cultural preservation, and community development laid the foundation for ongoing efforts to address Māori disparities and promote Māori rights in New Zealand.

Today, Te Puea Herangi is remembered as a visionary leader and an influential figure in Māori history. Her dedication to her people, her tireless advocacy, and her unwavering belief in the strength and resilience of Māori culture continue to inspire and guide the Māori community in their ongoing journey towards self-determination and cultural revitalization. Her legacy serves as a reminder of the power of leadership, compassion, and the pursuit of social justice.

The Battle of Gallipoli

The Battle of Gallipoli, also known as the Gallipoli Campaign, was a significant military campaign that took place during World War I. It was fought between the Allied forces, primarily made up of troops from the British Empire and France, and the Ottoman Empire.

The campaign aimed to capture the strategic Gallipoli Peninsula in modern-day Turkey, with the objective of gaining control of the Dardanelles Strait and ultimately securing a sea route to Russia. The Allies believed that a successful assault on Gallipoli would weaken the Ottoman Empire and potentially shorten the war.

The battle began on April 25, 1915, when Allied troops landed on the beaches of Gallipoli. However, they faced fierce resistance from well-entrenched Ottoman forces led by German military advisors. The rugged terrain, coupled with the Ottoman's determination to defend their homeland, made the campaign a grueling and protracted struggle.

The battle unfolded in a series of bloody and costly offensives, with both sides suffering heavy casualties. The Allies faced numerous challenges, including steep cliffs, barbed wire defenses, and the constant threat of Ottoman counterattacks. Despite their initial objectives, the Allies failed to make significant progress inland and were unable to break through the Ottoman lines.

The battle continued for eight months, characterized by intense fighting, trench warfare, and brutal conditions. Both sides endured significant losses, with estimates of over 130,000 casualties on the Allied side and over 80,000 casualties on the Ottoman side. The campaign was marked by a stalemate, with neither side able to achieve a decisive victory.

As the winter months approached, the Allies made the decision to withdraw their forces from Gallipoli. The evacuation, which took place between December 1915 and January 1916, was a challenging operation, as they had to withdraw their troops while avoiding detection by the Ottoman forces.

The Battle of Gallipoli had a profound impact on the countries involved and has since become a symbol of courage, sacrifice, and national identity. For the Allies, it was a costly and failed campaign that led to a reassessment of their strategies and a shift towards the Western Front. For the Ottoman Empire, it was a significant defensive victory that boosted morale and showcased their military capabilities.

Gallipoli holds a special place in the collective memory of Australia and New Zealand, as both countries suffered heavy losses during the campaign. Anzac Day, observed on April 25th each year, commemorates the landing of the Australian and New Zealand Army Corps (ANZAC) at Gallipoli and honors the bravery and sacrifice of all those who fought in the battle.

The Battle of Gallipoli remains a poignant reminder of the human cost of war and the challenges faced by soldiers in the face of adversity. It serves as a testament to the resilience, courage, and camaraderie displayed by troops on both sides and continues to be remembered as a significant event in world history.

The Hawaiian Renaissance

The Hawaiian Renaissance, also known as the Hawaiian Cultural Renaissance, was a significant cultural and political movement that emerged in the late 20th century in Hawaii. It marked a revitalization of Hawaiian cultural practices, language, arts, and identity, and played a crucial role in reclaiming and preserving Hawaiian heritage.

The Hawaiian Renaissance emerged as a response to the rapid Westernization and assimilation of Hawaiian culture that occurred during the 19th and early 20th centuries. The overthrow of the Hawaiian Kingdom in 1893 and subsequent annexation by the United States led to the suppression of Hawaiian language, traditions, and customs. This resulted in a loss of cultural identity and a decline in traditional practices.

In the 1960s and 1970s, a cultural awakening began to take hold among the Hawaiian people. There was a growing recognition of the importance of Hawaiian language, hula (traditional dance), music, and other cultural expressions as vital components of Hawaiian identity. This resurgence was fueled by a sense of pride, a desire to reconnect with ancestral roots, and a need to restore dignity to the Hawaiian people.

Key figures in the Hawaiian Renaissance movement included musicians, artists, activists, educators, and community leaders who worked tirelessly to promote Hawaiian culture and challenge the prevailing narrative that portrayed Hawaiian culture as primitive or inferior. They sought to instill a sense of cultural pride and promote the value of Hawaiian language, history, and arts.

One of the most influential aspects of the Hawaiian Renaissance was the revitalization of the Hawaiian language. Efforts were made to teach and promote the language in schools, communities, and cultural institutions. Hawaiian language immersion schools were established, helping to ensure the transmission of the language to future generations.

In addition to language revitalization, there was a resurgence of interest in traditional Hawaiian arts and crafts, such as hula, chant, carving, weaving, and navigation. Institutions like the Polynesian Voyaging Society spearheaded the revival of traditional voyaging and navigation techniques, using ancient Polynesian knowledge to navigate the Pacific Ocean without modern instruments.

The Hawaiian Renaissance also had significant political implications. It played a pivotal role in the resurgence of Hawaiian sovereignty movements and efforts to restore political autonomy to the Hawaiian people. Advocacy for Hawaiian rights, land restoration, and cultural preservation became central to the broader movement for social justice and indigenous rights.

The impact of the Hawaiian Renaissance continues to be felt in Hawaii today. Hawaiian language is taught in schools, traditional practices are celebrated, and cultural festivals and events showcase the richness of Hawaiian arts and traditions. The Renaissance has contributed to a greater appreciation and understanding of Hawaiian culture both within the islands and worldwide.

The Hawaiian Renaissance stands as a testament to the resilience, creativity, and determination of the Hawaiian people to reclaim their cultural heritage and assert their identity. It has fostered a sense of pride and unity among the Hawaiian community and serves as an inspiration for indigenous cultural revitalization movements around the world.

The Stolen Generations

The Stolen Generations refer to a dark chapter in Australian history that occurred between the late 1800s and the 1970s. It was a policy implemented by the Australian government and various state authorities that involved forcibly removing Aboriginal and Torres Strait Islander children from their families and communities. The aim was to assimilate these children into white society, severing their ties to their Indigenous culture, language, and heritage.

The justification for the removals was based on misguided beliefs of racial superiority, assimilationist ideologies, and the misguided belief that removing Indigenous children from their families would improve their lives. It was believed that removing them from their cultural roots and placing them in institutions or with white families would lead to their "civilizing" and integration into mainstream society.

Children were often taken by force, coercion, or deceit, with government officials, police, and welfare authorities playing a significant role in the removal process. Indigenous families were often given no say or choice in the matter, and children were taken without consideration for their well-being or the lifelong trauma it would inflict upon them and their families.

The impact of the Stolen Generations has been profound and enduring. The forced removals caused deep and lasting pain, trauma, and loss for the affected individuals, families, and communities. Children were stripped of their cultural identity, denied the opportunity to learn their language and traditions, and were often subjected to abuse, neglect, and discrimination in their new environments.

The policy of forced removal also had long-lasting social, cultural, and economic consequences for Indigenous communities. It contributed to the breakdown of families, the loss of intergenerational knowledge, and the erosion of cultural practices and traditions. Many Indigenous people continue to suffer the effects of intergenerational trauma resulting from the forced removals.

Recognition and acknowledgment of the Stolen Generations have been significant steps towards reconciliation in Australia. In 2008, the Australian government issued a formal apology to the Stolen Generations, acknowledging the injustice, pain, and suffering they endured. This apology was a pivotal moment in the healing process and a commitment to addressing the ongoing impacts of the policies.

Efforts are ongoing to support healing, reconciliation, and the restoration of Indigenous culture and identity. Programs have been implemented to provide support services for survivors and their families, to promote cultural revitalization, and to strengthen Indigenous self-determination and decision-making.

The Stolen Generations represent a profound violation of human rights and a shameful chapter in Australian history. The legacy of this policy continues to shape the experiences and struggles of Indigenous people today. It serves as a reminder of the importance of reconciliation, justice, and the need to address the ongoing inequalities faced by Aboriginal and Torres Strait Islander communities.

The Kiribati Dancers

The Kiribati Dancers are a vibrant and captivating group of performers who showcase the traditional dances and cultural heritage of the Republic of Kiribati, a small island nation in the Pacific Ocean. Their dances are an integral part of Kiribati's identity and are deeply rooted in the country's rich history, customs, and beliefs.

Kiribati, pronounced "kee-ree-bahss," consists of a scattered group of islands known as atolls. The dances of Kiribati are closely tied to the rhythms of the ocean, the land, and the daily life of its people. Through their movements, costumes, and music, the Kiribati Dancers tell stories of their ancestors, celebrate important events, and express their connection to the natural world.

One of the most iconic dances performed by the Kiribati Dancers is the Te Karanga, also known as the "Kiribati welcome dance." This dance is performed to greet visitors and symbolizes the warm hospitality of the Kiribati people. It involves rhythmic movements of the arms, legs, and body, accompanied by chants and songs.

Another popular dance is the Bubuti, a lively and energetic dance performed during celebrations and festivals. The dancers showcase their agility and skill as they move in sync, often incorporating elements of acrobatics and footwork. The Bubuti dance is accompanied by vibrant drum beats and the joyful voices of the dancers.

The Kiribati Dancers' performances are a visual spectacle, with dancers adorned in traditional attire. Men often wear colorful skirts made of pandanus leaves or rito, while women wear colorful dresses called te ira. Elaborate headdresses, necklaces, and woven accessories complete their ensemble, adding to the visual splendor of the performance.

Beyond their artistic expression, the Kiribati Dancers play an important role in preserving and promoting Kiribati culture. Through their performances, they pass down traditional dance techniques, songs, and stories to younger generations. They also serve as cultural ambassadors, showcasing Kiribati's unique heritage to audiences around the world.

The dances of Kiribati are more than just entertainment; they are a representation of the resilience, pride, and spirit of the Kiribati people. Despite the challenges they face, including climate change and rising sea levels that threaten their islands, the Kiribati Dancers continue to inspire and uplift through their passionate performances.

Whether performing at local festivals, cultural events, or on international stages, the Kiribati Dancers bring the spirit of Kiribati to life. Their vibrant dances, rhythmic movements, and infectious energy captivate audiences and serve as a reminder of the beauty and diversity of the Pacific culture. The Kiribati Dancers are cultural treasures, embodying the traditions and dreams of their people and ensuring that the dances of Kiribati continue to thrive for generations to come.

The Bougainville Civil War

The Bougainville Civil War was a conflict that took place on the island of Bougainville in Papua New Guinea between 1988 and 1998. It was a complex and protracted conflict rooted in issues of land rights, resource exploitation, and political autonomy.

The conflict began when local landowners, predominantly from the indigenous Bougainville population, raised concerns over the environmental and social impacts of the Panguna copper mine, operated by the Australian-owned Bougainville Copper Limited (BCL). The mine had been a significant source of revenue for Papua New Guinea but had caused extensive environmental damage and social disruption on Bougainville.

The Bougainville Revolutionary Army (BRA), led by Francis Ona, emerged as a militant group representing the interests of the landowners and seeking greater autonomy for Bougainville. They launched attacks on the mine and the Papua New Guinea security forces, triggering a cycle of violence and retaliation.

The conflict escalated over the years, with both the Papua New Guinea Defense Force (PNGDF) and the BRA engaging in guerilla warfare, sabotage, and human rights abuses. The PNGDF imposed a blockade on Bougainville, cutting off essential supplies, leading to a humanitarian crisis on the island.

Attempts at mediation and peace talks were made throughout the conflict, but a resolution proved elusive. In 1997, a ceasefire was brokered, leading to the negotiation of the Bougainville Peace Agreement in 2001. The agreement granted autonomy to Bougainville and established a process for a referendum on independence, which took place in 2019.

The Bougainville Civil War had significant human, social, and economic costs. Estimates suggest that between 15,000 and 20,000 people lost their lives during the conflict, and many more were displaced from their homes. The environmental damage caused by the mine and the blockade's impact on the local population's livelihoods were severe and long-lasting.

The Bougainville Peace Agreement paved the way for a peaceful resolution to the conflict, and in 2019, the majority of Bougainvilleans voted in favor of independence in the referendum. The process of negotiating the terms of independence is ongoing, with Papua New Guinea and Bougainville working towards a mutually agreed-upon outcome.

The Bougainville Civil War remains a significant chapter in the history of Papua New Guinea and Bougainville, highlighting the complexities of resource extraction, land rights, and self-determination. It serves as a reminder of the importance of peaceful dialogue, respect for human rights, and inclusive governance in addressing underlying grievances and building sustainable peace.

The Rise of Moana

"The Rise of Moana" is a captivating tale that takes us on a journey of discovery, bravery, and self-empowerment. Set in the enchanting world of Polynesia, the story follows the courageous young heroine Moana as she embarks on a quest to save her people and restore the balance of nature.

Moana, a spirited young woman from the island of Motunui, has always felt a deep connection to the ocean, despite her father's fears and the strict rules of her island. When a darkness threatens their land and their way of life, Moana sets out on a daring adventure to find the demigod Maui and seek his help in restoring the heart of Te Fiti, a powerful stone that holds the key to saving her people.

As Moana sails across the vast ocean, she encounters a series of challenges and discovers the true power within herself. Along the way, she forms an unlikely bond with the shape-shifting Maui, who teaches her valuable lessons about identity, bravery, and the importance of following one's own path. Moana's determination and resilience inspire those around her as she confronts her fears, embraces her heritage, and takes on the responsibility of being a leader.

The film beautifully showcases the rich cultural traditions and mythology of the Pacific Islands, celebrating the music, language, and customs of the Polynesian people. Through stunning animation, memorable songs, and heartfelt storytelling, "The Rise of Moana" captures the essence of the Pacific culture and offers a message of empowerment and self-discovery.

Moana's journey is not just a physical one but also a personal and emotional transformation. She learns to trust her instincts, listen to her heart, and embrace her role as a wayfinder, a navigator who charts her own course. Her story resonates with audiences of all ages, reminding us of the importance of staying true to ourselves, honoring our roots, and standing up for what we believe in.

"The Rise of Moana" is not just a story about a young girl's heroic journey but also a celebration of the power of determination, the beauty of cultural heritage, and the importance of protecting our environment. It encourages us to explore our own passions, seek our own truths, and discover the strength within us to make a difference in the world.

Through Moana's triumphs and challenges, we are reminded that anyone, regardless of age or background, can rise above adversity, find their purpose, and make a positive impact. Her story inspires us to embark on our own personal voyages of self-discovery, embracing the unknown with courage and embracing the power of our own voices. The rise of Moana represents the rise of our own potential, reminding us that we all have the ability to be heroes in our own lives.

The Miraculous Recovery of Ratu Sir Kamisese Mara

Ratu Sir Kamisese Mara, known as the "Father of the Nation" in Fiji, led an extraordinary life that was marked by his pivotal role in shaping the country's political landscape. However, it was his miraculous recovery from a near-fatal illness that truly captivated the nation and left a lasting impact on the people of Fiji.

Ratu Sir Kamisese Mara, a charismatic and respected leader, served as Fiji's Prime Minister and later as its President for many years. His political career was marked by his commitment to national unity, promoting cultural diversity, and advocating for the rights of indigenous Fijians.

In 1982, while still serving as the Prime Minister, Ratu Mara fell critically ill and was diagnosed with a severe heart condition. His condition deteriorated rapidly, and it seemed that the nation would lose one of its most beloved and influential leaders.

However, against all odds, Ratu Mara experienced a miraculous recovery that astounded the medical community and the people of Fiji. It was a turning point that captured the nation's attention and brought a renewed sense of hope and inspiration.

The news of Ratu Mara's recovery spread like wildfire, and people from all walks of life rejoiced in his resilience and determination. His return to health was seen as a testament to the strength and indomitable spirit of the Fijian people.

Following his recovery, Ratu Mara continued to lead Fiji with a renewed sense of purpose and dedication. He implemented numerous reforms, fostered economic development, and worked towards reconciliation among various ethnic communities in the country.

Ratu Mara's miraculous recovery became a symbol of hope and resilience for the people of Fiji. It served as a reminder that even in the face of adversity, there is always room for healing, growth, and transformation.

His story continues to inspire individuals to overcome challenges, persevere through difficult times, and embrace the power of the human spirit. Ratu Mara's legacy as a statesman, leader, and survivor lives on, serving as a reminder that miracles can happen, and that hope can triumph over despair.

The miraculous recovery of Ratu Sir Kamisese Mara stands as a testament to the power of faith, determination, and the unwavering spirit of a nation. It serves as a source of inspiration for the people of Fiji and a reminder of the incredible capacity of the human body and mind to overcome seemingly insurmountable obstacles.

The Rainbow Warrior

The Rainbow Warrior holds a significant place in the history of environmental activism as a symbol of peaceful protest and the fight for conservation. This iconic ship, operated by the environmental organization Greenpeace, played a crucial role in raising awareness about environmental issues and advocating for a sustainable future.

The Rainbow Warrior was originally built as a trawler in 1955, but it was acquired by Greenpeace in 1977 and transformed into a campaigning vessel. Its name, inspired by a Native American prophecy, represented the harmony between humans and nature. The ship became a beacon of hope and a powerful symbol for environmental activism worldwide.

One of the most notable events in the Rainbow Warrior's history took place in 1985 when it was preparing to protest against French nuclear testing in the Pacific. While docked in Auckland, New Zealand, the ship was targeted by a sabotage operation orchestrated by the French intelligence agency. Two explosive devices were planted on the ship, resulting in a tragic loss of life. Photographer Fernando Pereira, who was onboard capturing the campaign, lost his life in the explosion.

Despite this devastating event, the Rainbow Warrior's story did not end. Greenpeace received worldwide support, and the incident shed light on the importance of environmental activism. The ship's legacy continued, as a new Rainbow Warrior was commissioned and launched in 1989, continuing its mission to protect the environment and promote sustainable practices.

Throughout its history, the Rainbow Warrior has played a pivotal role in various environmental campaigns. It has protested against whaling, deforestation, climate change, and the use of nuclear power. The ship's crew, known as "Rainbow Warriors," have engaged in direct action, peaceful protests, and advocacy, drawing attention to pressing environmental issues and demanding change.

The Rainbow Warrior represents a spirit of activism, resilience, and determination. It has inspired individuals and communities to take action, stand up for what they believe in, and strive for a sustainable and just future. The ship's vibrant colors and powerful presence have become synonymous with environmental activism, reminding us of the urgent need to protect our planet and the interconnectedness of all living beings.

The legacy of the Rainbow Warrior extends beyond its physical presence. It symbolizes the ongoing fight for environmental justice, the power of grassroots movements, and the importance of individuals and organizations coming together to create positive change. The Rainbow Warrior serves as a constant reminder that every action, no matter how small, has the potential to make a significant impact and shape the future of our planet.

As we look to the future, the Rainbow Warrior's message remains as relevant as ever. It encourages us to take responsibility for the Earth and its resources, to challenge unsustainable practices, and to protect the biodiversity and beauty of our planet for generations to come. The Rainbow Warrior stands as a symbol of hope, reminding us that together, we can make a difference and create a world where humans and nature coexist in harmony.

The Story of Parihaka

The story of Parihaka is a significant and inspiring chapter in New Zealand's history, characterized by the peaceful resistance of the indigenous Māori people against unjust land confiscation and colonization. Located in Taranaki, Parihaka was a Māori village that became a symbol of nonviolent resistance and cultural resilience in the late 19th century.

Under the leadership of visionary leaders Te Whiti o Rongomai and Tohu Kākahi, Parihaka became a gathering place for Māori from various tribes seeking refuge from land seizures and encroachment by European settlers. Te Whiti and Tohu believed in peaceful protest and sought to protect the rights of Māori to their ancestral lands.

The movement at Parihaka advocated for passive resistance, encouraging Māori to peacefully resist the confiscation of their lands through acts such as plowing and cultivating disputed lands and refusing to engage in violent confrontation. Their philosophy centered on the principles of compassion, unity, and nonviolence, drawing inspiration from the teachings of Māori spiritual traditions.

The village of Parihaka grew in size and became a center for Māori cultural and political activities. It welcomed people from different tribes and became a hub of artistic expression, education, and community building. Parihaka's influence extended beyond Taranaki, reaching indigenous communities throughout New Zealand and inspiring movements around the world.

However, the peaceful resistance of Parihaka faced harsh opposition from the colonial government. In 1881, armed forces were sent to suppress the movement, resulting in the invasion and destruction of the village. Te Whiti and Tohu were arrested and imprisoned without trial, and many Māori were forcibly removed from their homes and lands.

Despite the hardships faced by the people of Parihaka, their spirit remained unbroken. They continued to advocate for justice and reconciliation, emphasizing the importance of forgiveness and unity in moving forward. In the years that followed, Parihaka became a symbol of the enduring strength and resilience of Māori culture.

Today, Parihaka stands as a place of remembrance and reflection, serving as a powerful reminder of the consequences of colonialism and the importance of cultural preservation. The story of Parihaka inspires ongoing efforts for land rights, cultural revitalization, and reconciliation between Māori and the wider New Zealand society.

The legacy of Parihaka resonates in contemporary New Zealand, where there is a growing recognition of the injustices faced by Māori and a commitment to honoring the Treaty of Waitangi, which guarantees the rights and wellbeing of the indigenous people. Parihaka continues to be a site of pilgrimage and a symbol of hope, reminding people of the power of peaceful resistance, cultural pride, and the pursuit of justice.

The Aboriginal Art Movement

The Aboriginal Art Movement is a cultural and artistic movement that has had a profound impact on the art world and serves as a powerful expression of Indigenous Australian identity and heritage. Rooted in the rich traditions and spirituality of Aboriginal culture, this movement has provided a platform for artists to tell their stories, preserve their cultural knowledge, and challenge misconceptions about Indigenous peoples.

Aboriginal art is deeply connected to the land, Dreamtime stories, and ancestral teachings. It encompasses a wide range of artistic forms, including paintings, sculptures, rock art, bark paintings, and contemporary installations. Traditional techniques, such as dot painting, cross-hatching, and ochre pigments, are often employed, symbolizing a connection to the land and ancestral spirits.

The movement gained significant momentum during the late 20th century when Aboriginal artists began to receive recognition and demand for their artwork grew both locally and internationally. One of the pivotal moments was the establishment of the Papunya Tula art movement in the 1970s in the remote community of Papunya in Central Australia. This movement, led by artists such as Clifford Possum Tjapaltjarri and Emily Kame Kngwarreye, played a vital role in bringing Aboriginal art to a global audience.

Aboriginal art is characterized by its diversity, reflecting the multitude of Aboriginal cultures and languages across Australia. Each artwork tells a story, often representing ancestral journeys, sacred sites, spiritual beliefs, or personal experiences. The intricate patterns, vibrant colors, and symbology used in the artwork serve as a visual language, connecting the viewer with the spiritual and cultural significance of the piece.

The Aboriginal Art Movement has not only provided a means of artistic expression but has also brought social and economic benefits to Indigenous communities. It has created opportunities for cultural revitalization, cultural pride, and economic empowerment. Aboriginal-owned art cooperatives and galleries have emerged, allowing artists to showcase their work, earn income, and maintain control over their cultural heritage.

Today, Aboriginal art is celebrated and collected around the world, with exhibitions and galleries dedicated to showcasing the diverse talent of Aboriginal artists. It has transcended boundaries and challenged stereotypes, influencing contemporary art practices and shaping global conversations about Indigenous rights, cultural preservation, and reconciliation.

The Aboriginal Art Movement continues to thrive, with new generations of artists exploring innovative techniques, themes, and materials while staying grounded in the traditions and stories passed down through generations. It serves as a powerful force for cultural preservation, self-expression, and cross-cultural understanding, fostering a deeper appreciation and respect for the rich heritage and contributions of Australia's First Nations peoples.

The Story Bridge Adventure Climb

The Story Bridge Adventure Climb is a thrilling and unique experience that allows visitors to climb Brisbane's iconic Story Bridge and enjoy breathtaking panoramic views of the city and its surroundings. Located in Queensland, Australia, the Story Bridge is not only an engineering marvel but also an iconic symbol of Brisbane's history and development.

The adventure climb offers participants the opportunity to scale the bridge's steel structure, ascending to a height of approximately 80 meters above the Brisbane River. Led by experienced climb leaders, participants are equipped with safety harnesses and given a comprehensive safety briefing before embarking on their journey.

As climbers make their way up the bridge, they are treated to spectacular views of the cityscape, including the Brisbane River, the central business district, and the surrounding natural beauty of the area. The climb also provides a unique vantage point to appreciate the architectural intricacies of the bridge itself, with its distinctive steel framework and suspension cables.

Throughout the climb, knowledgeable climb leaders share fascinating stories and historical facts about the bridge and its significance to the city. Participants gain insights into the bridge's construction, its role in Brisbane's transportation system, and the cultural heritage associated with it.

The adventure climb caters to individuals of varying fitness levels, with different climb options available to suit different preferences. From a leisurely climb to a more challenging and adventurous journey, participants can choose the experience that best matches their abilities and comfort levels.

Safety is of utmost importance during the climb, with strict safety protocols and equipment checks in place to ensure a secure and enjoyable experience for all participants. Climbers are provided with all necessary gear, including helmets and harnesses, and are guided by experienced climb leaders who are trained to handle various climbing scenarios.

The Story Bridge Adventure Climb offers a truly unforgettable experience, allowing participants to not only conquer the heights but also gain a unique perspective on the city of Brisbane. Whether it's a solo adventure, a family outing, or a team-building activity, the climb provides a sense of achievement, exhilaration, and an opportunity to create lasting memories.

Beyond the adventure itself, the climb also contributes to the preservation and maintenance of the iconic Story Bridge. The fees from the climb help fund ongoing bridge maintenance and conservation efforts, ensuring that this historical landmark continues to be enjoyed by locals and visitors alike for generations to come.

The Story Bridge Adventure Climb is an adventure seekers' delight, offering an extraordinary opportunity to witness the beauty of Brisbane from a new perspective while immersing oneself in the history and grandeur of the iconic Story Bridge. It is an experience that combines adrenaline, knowledge, and stunning views, making it a must-try activity for those visiting the vibrant city of Brisbane.

The Maori Battalion

The Maori Battalion, also known as the 28th Maori Battalion, was a highly esteemed and respected military unit comprised primarily of Maori soldiers from New Zealand during World War II. The battalion played a significant role in various campaigns and engagements, earning a reputation for their bravery, resilience, and unwavering commitment to their country.

The formation of the Maori Battalion was a result of the New Zealand government's decision to establish a unit specifically for Maori soldiers in 1940. The goal was to provide an opportunity for Maori men to contribute to the war effort and showcase their skills and dedication to their homeland. The battalion drew its recruits from different iwi (tribes) across New Zealand, fostering a sense of unity and camaraderie among its members.

From 1940 to 1945, the Maori Battalion served in several theaters of war, including North Africa, Greece, Crete, and Italy. They fought alongside Allied forces, engaging in intense combat and enduring harsh conditions. The battalion's soldiers displayed exceptional courage and resourcefulness, often going beyond the call of duty to protect their comrades and achieve their objectives.

The Maori Battalion's strong cultural identity and traditions played a crucial role in their military operations. They performed the haka, a traditional Maori war dance, to intimidate their enemies and boost their own morale. The haka became a symbol of the battalion's indomitable spirit and helped forge a strong bond among its members.

Throughout their service, the Maori Battalion faced many challenges, including racism and discrimination. Despite these obstacles, they remained steadfast in their commitment to their country and their determination to prove themselves as capable and courageous soldiers. The battalion's exemplary performance earned them respect and admiration from both their comrades and their adversaries.

The Maori Battalion's achievements were not limited to the battlefield. They also played a vital role in fostering cultural pride and promoting Maori culture during the war. They organized cultural performances, established Maori clubs, and actively engaged with local communities wherever they were stationed. Their efforts helped to raise awareness and appreciation for Maori culture, both within the military and among the wider population.

After the war, the legacy of the Maori Battalion continued to inspire future generations. Their bravery and sacrifices served as a testament to the courage and resilience of the Maori people. The battalion's contribution to New Zealand's war effort and its impact on Maori identity and pride are widely recognized and celebrated.

Today, the memory of the Maori Battalion lives on through various commemorative activities and events. Their stories and achievements are passed down through oral traditions, documentaries, books, and museums, ensuring that their legacy remains a source of inspiration and pride for all New Zealanders.

The Maori Battalion's service in World War II not only demonstrated their bravery and valor but also contributed to the broader struggle for equality and recognition of Maori rights. Their legacy serves as a reminder of the important role that indigenous peoples have played in shaping the history and identity of New Zealand.

The Haka

The Haka is a traditional Māori war dance that holds great cultural significance for the Māori people of New Zealand. It is a powerful and energetic performance characterized by vigorous movements, rhythmic chanting, and fierce facial expressions. The Haka serves various purposes, including as a form of cultural expression, a means of communication, and a way to honor ancestors and celebrate significant events.

The origins of the Haka can be traced back to the early Māori tribes, where it was performed as a prelude to battle. It was used to intimidate enemies, boost the morale of warriors, and invoke the spirits of ancestors for protection and guidance. The Haka was a way for Māori warriors to display their strength, courage, and unity before engaging in combat.

Today, the Haka is performed on various occasions, both within Māori communities and by New Zealanders of all backgrounds. It is commonly seen at cultural events, sporting matches, ceremonies, and other significant gatherings. The most well-known Haka is called "Ka Mate," which was composed by Ngāti Toa chief Te Rauparaha in the early 19th century.

The Haka is characterized by its rhythmic movements, synchronized foot stomping, and forceful gestures. The performers use their bodies, hands, and facial expressions to convey different emotions and tell stories. The chanting and shouting, accompanied by gestures like sticking out tongues and slapping chests, are intended to demonstrate strength, unity, and defiance.

The Haka holds deep cultural significance for Māori people and is an important aspect of their identity and heritage. It represents their connection to the land, their ancestors, and their shared history. It is also a way to express pride in Māori culture and to pass on traditions and knowledge to younger generations.

In addition to its cultural significance, the Haka has gained international recognition and popularity. The New Zealand national rugby team, known as the All Blacks, performs a Haka called "Ka Mate" before their matches. This iconic display of the Haka has become synonymous with the team and is widely recognized around the world.

The Haka's unique combination of physical movements, chanting, and expressions of strength and unity make it a captivating and awe-inspiring performance. It serves as a powerful symbol of Māori culture, resilience, and pride. Through the Haka, the Māori people continue to preserve their traditions, connect with their heritage, and share their rich cultural heritage with the world.

The Sydney Opera House

The Sydney Opera House is one of the most iconic architectural landmarks in the world, located in Sydney, Australia. It is renowned for its distinctive sail-shaped roofs and stunning waterfront setting. Designed by Danish architect Jørn Utzon, the Sydney Opera House has become a symbol of both the city and the country, attracting millions of visitors each year.

Construction of the Sydney Opera House began in 1959 and took over 14 years to complete, officially opening its doors in 1973. The design of the building was a revolutionary feat of engineering and construction, utilizing innovative techniques and materials. The unique sail-like shells that make up the roof were inspired by Utzon's vision of mimicking the natural shapes of seashells.

The Sydney Opera House is not just a single venue but a complex comprising multiple performance spaces, including the Concert Hall, Opera Theatre, Drama Theatre, Playhouse, and Studio. These spaces cater to a wide range of performances, including opera, ballet, theater, music concerts, and more. The Concert Hall, with its impressive organ and seating capacity of over 2,000, is the largest and most prestigious venue within the Opera House.

Beyond its architectural marvel, the Sydney Opera House has played a significant role in shaping the cultural landscape of Australia. It has become a hub for artistic expression, hosting a diverse array of performances from both local and international artists. The Opera House has also been a catalyst for the development of Sydney's vibrant arts and entertainment scene.

The Sydney Opera House's significance extends beyond its artistic and cultural contributions. In 2007, it was recognized as a UNESCO World Heritage site, highlighting its outstanding universal value and importance to humanity. Its design and engineering innovations have influenced generations of architects and designers worldwide.

The Sydney Opera House is not only a cultural institution but also an important symbol of Australian identity and pride. Its distinctive silhouette has become synonymous with the city of Sydney and is often featured in travel brochures, postcards, and advertisements promoting Australia as a tourist destination.

Visitors to the Sydney Opera House can not only enjoy world-class performances but also explore its stunning interiors, take guided tours, dine at its restaurants and bars, and soak in the breathtaking views of Sydney Harbour. The site also hosts various festivals and events throughout the year, further enhancing its role as a vibrant cultural hub.

In conclusion, the Sydney Opera House stands as an architectural masterpiece, an artistic haven, and a symbol of national pride. Its unique design, cultural significance, and breathtaking location make it an enduring symbol of Australia's rich artistic and architectural heritage.

The Kokoda Track

The Kokoda Track is a historic and challenging trail located in Papua New Guinea. It holds significant historical and cultural importance as it was the site of the Kokoda Campaign during World War II. The track stretches for approximately 96 kilometers (60 miles) through rugged and dense jungle terrain, crossing the Owen Stanley Range.

During the Kokoda Campaign, which took place from July to November 1942, Australian forces fought against the Japanese army in a series of intense battles along the Kokoda Track. The track served as a crucial supply route and a strategic point in the defense of Port Moresby, the capital of Papua New Guinea. The campaign marked a turning point in the Pacific War and is considered a significant part of Australia's military history.

Today, the Kokoda Track attracts adventurers, history enthusiasts, and trekkers from around the world who seek to experience the physical and emotional challenges of retracing the footsteps of the soldiers who fought there. The trek offers a unique opportunity to connect with history, pay tribute to the fallen, and gain a deeper understanding of the sacrifices made during the war.

The Kokoda Track is renowned for its demanding terrain, with steep inclines, muddy paths, river crossings, and dense vegetation. Trekkers must be physically fit and mentally prepared for the arduous journey, which typically takes around 7 to 10 days to complete. Along the track, there are several significant landmarks, including battle sites, war memorials, and villages that provide insight into the local culture and way of life.

The trek along the Kokoda Track is not only a physical challenge but also an opportunity for personal reflection and growth. Many trekkers report being deeply moved by the history, the beauty of the natural surroundings, and the encounters with local communities along the way. The experience fosters a sense of camaraderie and resilience, as trekkers face the same physical and emotional hardships that the soldiers endured.

The Kokoda Track holds a special place in the hearts of Australians and Papua New Guineans, symbolizing the spirit of sacrifice, endurance, and resilience. It is a living memorial to those who fought and lost their lives in the Kokoda Campaign, and it serves as a reminder of the importance of remembering and honoring their legacy.

In recent years, efforts have been made to improve the infrastructure along the track, including the establishment of campsites, toilets, and bridges, making it more accessible to trekkers while also ensuring the preservation of its historical and environmental significance.

In conclusion, the Kokoda Track is not just a physical trail; it is a journey that immerses trekkers in the history and culture of Papua New Guinea and pays tribute to the bravery and sacrifices of the soldiers who fought during the Kokoda Campaign. It is a challenging yet rewarding experience that allows visitors to connect with the past and gain a deeper appreciation for the enduring human spirit.

The Healing Power of Wai Ora

Wai Ora, which translates to "water of life" in the Māori language, refers to the healing power of water in traditional Māori culture. Water holds significant spiritual and medicinal importance for the Māori people, who believe in its ability to restore balance and promote well-being.

In Māori traditions, water is seen as a sacred element that connects humans to the natural world and the spiritual realm. It is believed to have the power to cleanse, purify, and revitalize both the body and the spirit. The healing properties of water are deeply ingrained in Māori cultural practices and rituals.

Wai Ora encompasses various forms of water healing, including wai tapu (sacred water) and wai Māori (traditional Māori water). These practices involve using water in ceremonies, baths, and therapeutic treatments to promote physical, emotional, and spiritual healing.

One of the most well-known examples of Wai Ora is the traditional Māori steam bath, known as a rongoā or mirimiri. This therapeutic practice involves using steam infused with medicinal herbs and plants to cleanse the body, release toxins, and promote relaxation and healing. The steam bath is often accompanied by chants, prayers, and other rituals that enhance the spiritual and healing experience.

In addition to steam baths, Māori healing practices also include immersion in natural bodies of water, such as rivers, lakes, and hot springs. These natural water sources are believed to possess unique healing properties, with each having its own distinct energy and therapeutic benefits. The Māori people have long utilized these natural resources for their healing properties, seeking solace and rejuvenation in the waters.

The healing power of Wai Ora extends beyond the physical realm. It is also deeply connected to the cultural and spiritual identity of the Māori people. Water is considered a taonga (treasure) and a source of life, symbolizing the interconnectedness of all living beings and the need for balance and harmony.

In recent years, the concept of Wai Ora has gained recognition beyond Māori culture and has been embraced as a holistic approach to well-being and healing. Spas and wellness centers in New Zealand and around the world now offer Wai Ora-inspired treatments that incorporate Māori healing practices and philosophies.

The healing power of Wai Ora serves as a reminder of the importance of reconnecting with nature, embracing traditional wisdom, and nurturing the mind, body, and spirit. It is a testament to the profound wisdom and knowledge of the Māori people, who have long understood the therapeutic and transformative qualities of water.

The Fire-Walking Ritual of Beqa Island

The fire-walking ritual of Beqa Island is a fascinating and awe-inspiring tradition that has been passed down through generations in the Fijian culture. Located in the South Pacific, Beqa Island is renowned for its fire-walking ceremony, known as "vilavilairevo," which translates to "jumping into the oven."

The fire-walking ritual holds deep spiritual and cultural significance for the people of Beqa Island. It is believed to have originated centuries ago when a warrior named Tui Namoliwai demonstrated his bravery by walking across hot stones to prove his loyalty to the Fijian king. Since then, fire-walking has become a symbol of courage, strength, and spiritual connection for the islanders.

The ceremony takes place in a specially prepared pit, known as a "bega," which is filled with smoldering hot stones. These stones are heated for several hours using a traditional method involving coconut husks, which create intense heat. The fire-walkers, known as "vilavilairevo," undergo a period of purification and preparation before the event, which includes fasting, prayer, and rituals performed by the village chief.

As the night falls and the atmosphere becomes charged with anticipation, the fire-walkers, adorned in traditional attire and accompanied by rhythmic chants and music, approach the fiery pit. With bare feet, they step onto the scorching stones, walking across the glowing embers without showing signs of pain or injury. The spectacle is both visually stunning and emotionally captivating, as the fire-walkers display immense bravery and spiritual connection.

The fire-walking ritual is believed to be a test of faith and a way to connect with ancestral spirits. It is considered a form of spiritual cleansing and a demonstration of the bond between the physical and spiritual worlds. The fire-walkers are revered as sacred figures, embodying the strength and protection of their ancestors.

The ritual of fire-walking in Beqa Island attracts visitors from around the world who come to witness this extraordinary event. It provides a unique opportunity to witness a living cultural tradition and experience the power of faith, resilience, and community unity.

The fire-walking ritual of Beqa Island serves as a testament to the enduring traditions and spiritual beliefs of the Fijian people. It is a celebration of courage, faith, and the indomitable spirit of the human experience.

A s we conclude our exploration of "Untamed Horizons: Extraordinary Tales of Oceania's Resilience, Diversity, and Wonder," we hope that this collection of remarkable case studies has left you inspired, enlightened, and deeply connected to the spirit of Oceania. Throughout these pages, we have witnessed the triumphs, challenges, and unwavering resilience of the people who call this region home.

From the courageous navigators who braved the vast Pacific Ocean, guided only by the stars and their ancestral knowledge, to the visionary leaders who have fought for indigenous rights and cultural preservation, Oceania's stories are a testament to the strength of human spirit. We have witnessed the awe-inspiring beauty of the region's landscapes, the richness of its traditions, and the profound wisdom embedded in its ancient cultures.

Through the tales of innovation, environmental stewardship, artistic expression, and social change, we have celebrated the diversity of Oceania and the remarkable individuals who have left an indelible mark on its history. These stories remind us of the importance of preserving cultural heritage, protecting the environment, and fostering inclusivity and respect for all.

As we bid farewell to this journey, we invite you to carry the spirit of Oceania with you. Let its stories inspire you to embrace resilience, honor diversity, and foster a deep connection to the wonders of our world. May the lessons learned from these extraordinary tales continue to shape our collective consciousness and guide us towards a future that respects and values the richness of our diverse planet.

Thank you for embarking on this unforgettable adventure through "Untamed Horizons: Extraordinary Tales of Oceania's Resilience, Diversity, and Wonder." May it serve as a reminder of the boundless potential that lies within each of us and the remarkable power of human stories to inspire, unite, and transform.